COLORS ON MY PLATE

Fruits and Vegetables

An interactive nutritional Guide for children

Deva Northon

Why is important to eat healthy?

Eating healthy is important for kids because it helps their bodies grow strong and stay healthy. Here are some reasons why eating healthy is important:

1. Energy Boost: Eating healthy foods like fruits, vegetables, whole grains, and lean proteins gives our bodies the energy they need to do all the things we love, like playing sports, running, and having fun with friends.
2. Strong Bones and Muscles: Healthy foods, especially foods rich in calcium like milk, cheese, and yogurt, help us build strong bones and teeth. Foods with protein, like lean meats, beans, and nuts, help us develop strong muscles.

3 .Growth and Development: When we eat a variety of healthy foods, it provides our bodies with the necessary vitamins and minerals that help us grow properly and develop in the right way. These nutrients are like building blocks that our bodies need to stay healthy.

4.Boosting the Immune System: Eating healthy foods helps to strengthen our immune system, which is like our body's defense system against germs and illnesses. Fruits and vegetables, for example, are packed with vitamins and antioxidants that help keep us healthy and fight off sickness.

5.Focus and Learning: When we eat healthy foods, it helps our brain function at its best. Foods like whole grains, fruits, and vegetables provide us with important nutrients that improve our memory, concentration, and overall brainpower. This helps us do better in school and learn new things.

6.Preventing Diseases: By eating healthy, we can lower the risk of developing certain diseases later in life, such as heart disease, diabetes, and some types of cancer. Eating lots of fruits, vegetables, and whole grains helps keep our bodies strong and protected.

Remember, eating healthy doesn't mean we can't enjoy treats and snacks once in a while. It's about making good choices most of the time and finding a balance. So, let's make sure to eat a rainbow of fruits and vegetables, drink plenty of water, and have a well-rounded diet to keep our bodies happy and healthy!

Why eating fruits and vegetables?

Here are some reasons why you should eat fruit and vegetables:

1. **Energy and Growing Strong**: Just like how a car needs fuel to run, our bodies need energy to do all the fun things we love to do, like playing sports, riding bikes, and jumping around. Fruits and vegetables are like the super fuel that gives our bodies the energy they need to grow big and strong.

2. Superhero Nutrients: Fruits and vegetables are packed with special nutrients that act like superheroes inside our bodies. They help keep us healthy and protect us from getting sick. These superheroes have names like vitamins, minerals, and antioxidants. They make our muscles strong, our bones healthy, and our skin shiny.

3. Bright Colors and Fun Flavors: Have you ever noticed how fruits and vegetables come in so many different colors? They're like a rainbow on your plate! Each color has a different superpower. For example, red fruits and veggies help our hearts stay healthy, orange ones are good for our immune system, and green ones make our bones strong. Plus, they taste yummy and can be crunchy, juicy, or sweet. It's like having a tasty adventure with every bite!

4. Happy Tummies and Potty Power: Fruits and vegetables are like the superheroes of our tummies too! They have a special ingredient called fiber that helps our tummies work properly and keeps everything moving smoothly. This means we won't feel yucky or get tummy aches. Fiber also helps us have super potty power by making sure we can easily go to the bathroom.

5. Super Snack Fun: Fruits and vegetables can be super fun to eat! You can have a fruit salad with your favorite fruits or try making veggie faces on your plate using colorful veggies like carrots, cucumbers, and cherry tomatoes. You can even have a contest with your friends or siblings to see who can eat the most different colors in a day.

Remember, when we eat fruits and vegetables, we're not just eating tasty and colorful food. We're also giving our bodies the special superpowers they need to stay healthy, grow strong, and have lots of energy for all the exciting things we do. So, let's enjoy our fruits and veggies and become superheroes ourselves!

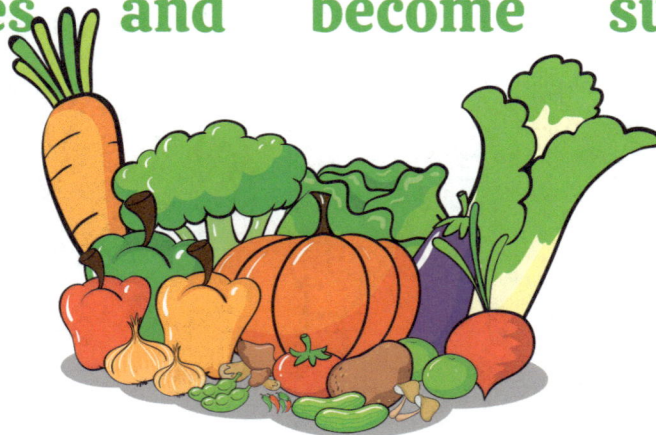

RED

Red fruits and vegetables support your immune system, and promote the health of your heart.

They contain:
- Lycopene – powerful antioxidant,
- Vitamin C – support the immune system,
- Beta – Carotene – Healthy Vision,
- Diverse Antioxidants: Healty Skin, healthy Digestive System, reduce Inflammation.

Watermelon

Tomato

Beet

Red Bell Pepper

Strawberry

Red fruits and vegetables

Red Apples

Strawberries

Raspberries

Cherries

Red Grapes

Watermelon

Pomegranate

Red Bell Peppers

Tomatoes

Cranberries

Red Onions

Beets

Radishes

Red Cabbage

Red Grapefruit

Which below belongs to red fruits group?

Write down or draw your red favourite fruits and vegetables.

 - - - - - - - - - - - - - - - -

 - - - - - - - - - - - - - - - -

 - - - - - - - - - - - - - - - -

 - - - - - - - - - - - - - - - -

 - - - - - - - - - - - - - - - -

 - - - - - - - - - - - - - - - -

 - - - - - - - - - - - - - - - -

Draw your Favorites

My Notes:

Challenge

Search, find and try a recipe that has a red fruit or veggie as ingredient.
Write it below!

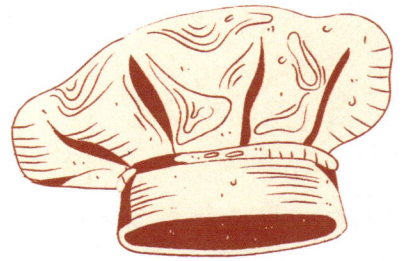

ORANGE

Orange fruits and vegetables are rich in vitamin C and beta-carotene, promoting healthy eyes, strong immune systems, and supporting your growth.

They contain:

- **Vitamin C Boost** – aids in wound healing, promotes the absorption of iron,
- **Nutrients, such as potassium, folate, and vitamin B6, which are important for children's growth, brain development, and overall health.**
- **Antioxidants** – protect cells from oxidative stress

Cantaloupe

Orange

Sweet Potato

Carrot

Papaya

Orange fruits and vegetables

Oranges
Carrots
Sweet Potatoes
Mangoes
Cantaloupes
Pumpkins
Apricots
Papayas
Persimmons

Butternut Squash
Orange Bell Peppers
Kumquats
Nectarines
Orange Tomatoes
Orange Cauliflower

Which below belongs to orange veggie´s group?

Write down or draw your orange favourite fruits and vegetables.

- ✓ _ _ _ _ _ _ _ _ _ _ _ _ _ _ _
- ✓ _ _ _ _ _ _ _ _ _ _ _ _ _ _ _
- ✓ _ _ _ _ _ _ _ _ _ _ _ _ _ _ _
- ✓ _ _ _ _ _ _ _ _ _ _ _ _ _ _ _
- ✓ _ _ _ _ _ _ _ _ _ _ _ _ _ _ _
- ✓ _ _ _ _ _ _ _ _ _ _ _ _ _ _ _
- ✓ _ _ _ _ _ _ _ _ _ _ _ _ _ _ _

Draw your Favorites

My Notes:

Challenge

Search, find and try a recipe that has an orange fruit or veggie as ingredient.
Write it below!

YELLOW

Yellow fruits and vegetables support healthy growth, boost immune function, and contribute to your eye health.

They contain:
- Natural sugars – provide you a quick source of energy,
- Tryptophan – help boost mood and promote feelings of well-being,
- Nutrient Variety – providing you a colorful and appetizing meal experience.

Onion

Lemon

Yellow Bell Pepper

Banana

Pineapple

Yellow fruits and vegetables

Bananas	Yellow Watermelon
Pineapples	Golden Kiwi
Yellow Apples	Yellow Peaches
Yellow Bell Peppers	Yellow Pears
Lemons	Yellow Corn
Yellow Squash	Yellow Beans
Yellow Tomatoes	Yellow Zucchini
	Yellow Cherries

Do you know the answer?

What vitamin is abundant in lemons, known for its immune-boosting properties?

Write down or draw your yellow favourite fruits and vegetables.

☑ - - - - - - - - - - - - - - - - - -

☑ - - - - - - - - - - - - - - - - - -

☑ - - - - - - - - - - - - - - - - - -

☑ - - - - - - - - - - - - - - - - - -

☑ - - - - - - - - - - - - - - - - - -

☑ - - - - - - - - - - - - - - - - - -

☑ - - - - - - - - - - - - - - - - - -

Draw your Favorites

My Notes:

Challenge

Search, find and try a recipe that has an yellow fruit or veggie as ingredient.
Write it below!

GREEN

Green fruits and vegetables provide you with essential vitamins, minerals, and fiber, supporting your healthy growth, strong bones, a robust immune system, and good digestion.

They contain:

- Rich in calcium and vitamin K, which contribute to strong bones and teeth,
- High in fiber, making them a healthy choice for managing your weight and promoting a balanced diet,
- High water content, contributing to your proper hydration and supporting overall bodily functions.

Kiwi

Broccoli

Cucumber

Spinach

Avocado

Green fruits and vegetables

Spinach	Zucchini
Green Apples	Green Beans
Broccoli	Cucumbers
Green Grapes	Green Pears
Kiwi	Green Tomatoes
Avocado	Brussels Sprouts
Green Bell Peppers	Green Cabbage
	Green Lentils

Did you know?

Did you know that green fruits like kiwi and green apples are not only delicious but also excellent sources of vitamin C? In fact, kiwis have even more vitamin C per serving than oranges! So, adding these green gems to your diet can give your immune system a powerful boost.

Write down or draw your green favourite fruits and vegetables.

- ✓ -------------------------
- ✓ -------------------------
- ✓ -------------------------
- ✓ -------------------------
- ✓ -------------------------
- ✓ -------------------------
- ✓ -------------------------

Draw your Favorites

My Notes

Challenge

Search, find and try a recipe that has a green fruit or veggie as ingredient.
Write it below!

BLUE

Blue fruits and vegetables are rich in antioxidants, promote your brain health, support memory function, and contribute to your overall cognitive development.

They contain:

- **Antioxidants Anthocyanins** – improve your brain function and memory retention, promoting cognitive health and supporting optimal brain development,
- **Nutrients Variety** – promoting your urinary tract health, preventing urinary tract infections, and supporting kidney function,
- **Vitamin , Lutein and Zeaxanthin** – help you in having a healthy vision.

Plums

Blueberries

Grapes

Blue fruits and vegetables

Blueberries
Blue Grapes
Blackberries (with bluish tint)
Elderberries (with bluish color)

True or False

Blueberries are packed with antioxidants that help protect against cell damage and promote overall health.

Write down or draw your blue favourite fruits and vegetables.

- ☑ - - - - - - - - - - - - - - - - - -
- ☑ - - - - - - - - - - - - - - - - - -
- ☑ - - - - - - - - - - - - - - - - - -
- ☑ - - - - - - - - - - - - - - - - - -
- ☑ - - - - - - - - - - - - - - - - - -
- ☑ - - - - - - - - - - - - - - - - - -
- ☑ - - - - - - - - - - - - - - - - - -

Draw your Favorites

My Notes:

Challenge
Search, find and try a recipe that has a blue fruit or veggie as ingredient.
Write it below!

PURPLE

Purple fruits and vegetables are rich in antioxidants, support a healthy immune system, promote brain health, and contribute to your overall well-being.

They contain:

- Powerful Antioxidants - such as Anthocyanins, which help protect against cell damage, reduce inflammation, and support your overall health,
- Compounds - to improve your cognitive function, memory, and overall brain health.
- Nutrients Variety -promoting healthier-looking skin and overall vitality. .

Onion

Dragon Fruit

Cabbage

Grapes

Eggplant

Purple fruits and vegetables

Eggplant
Purple Grapes
Plums
Blackberries
Purple Figs
Purple Passionfruit
Purple Cauliflower

Purple Asparagus
Purple Carrots (with purple flesh)
Purple Potatoes
Purple Cabbage
Purple Kale
Purple Sweet Potatoes
Purple Corn
Purple Radishes

True or False

Purple cabbage gets its vibrant color from anthocyanins, which are powerful antioxidants that help protect the body against cell damage and promote overall health.

Write down or draw your purple favourite fruits and vegetables.

☑ - - - - - - - - - - - - - - - - - -

☑ - - - - - - - - - - - - - - - - - -

☑ - - - - - - - - - - - - - - - - - -

☑ - - - - - - - - - - - - - - - - - -

☑ - - - - - - - - - - - - - - - - - -

☑ - - - - - - - - - - - - - - - - - -

☑ - - - - - - - - - - - - - - - - - -

Draw your Favorites

My Notes:

Challenge
Search, find and try a recipe that has a purple fruit or veggie as ingredient.
Write it below!

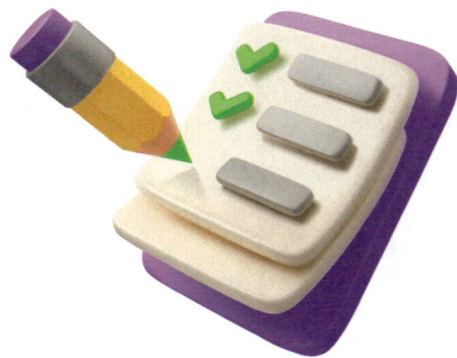

1. Test your knowledge

1. True or False: Eating fruits and vegetables can help keep us healthy and protect us from getting sick:
A.
F.

2. Which nutrient is abundant in oranges and helps boost our immune system?
a) Vitamin C
b) Calcium
c) Iron

3. Which colored fruits and vegetables are good for our eyesight?
a) Purple
b) Yellow
c) Green

Test your knowledge

4.True or False: Fiber in fruits and vegetables helps our digestion and prevents constipation.
A.
F.

5.Which nutrient found in blueberries promotes brain health and memory function?
a) Vitamin A
b) Anthocyanins
c) Vitamin D

Answers:

1.True
2. a) Vitamin C
3. b) Yellow
4.True
5. b) Anthocyanins

2. Test your knowledge

1.True or False: Vegetables are a good source of essential vitamins and minerals.

A.

F.

2Which vegetable is known for its high vitamin C content? a) Spinach

b) Carrot

c) Broccoli

d) Bell pepper

3.Fill in the blank: Eating a variety of vegetables can help improve _____.

4. True or False: Vegetables are low in calories and can aid in weight management.

A.

F.

Test your knowledge

5.Which vegetable is a good source of dietary fiber?
 a) Cauliflower
 b) Cucumber
 c) Sweet potato
 d) Green peas

6.Fill in the blank: Vegetables are rich in _____, which are beneficial for maintaining a healthy digestive system.

7.True or False: Vegetables are known to have antioxidant properties, which can help fight against certain diseases.
A.
F.

8.Which vegetable is high in potassium?
a) Mushroom
b) Zucchini
c) Eggplant
d) Tomato

Test your knowledge

9. Fill in the blank: Regular consumption of vegetables can contribute to overall _____ health.

10. True or False: Including a variety of vegetables in your diet can help reduce the risk of chronic diseases.

Answers:

10. True
9. Overall
8. d) Tomato
7. True
6. Fiber
5. e) Sweet potato
4. True
3. Overall health
2. d) Bell pepper
1. True